Dear Bob —
May tulips always bloom
in your Garden!
                    The Leys
2005

Tulips

Introduction by Scott D. Appell

MetroBooks

INTRODUCTION

Tulips in a bouquet convey the message of fame.
Red tulips in a bouquet convey the message of a declaration of love.
Variegated tulips in a bouquet convey the message of beautiful eyes.
Yellow tulips in a bouquet convey the message of hopeless love.

KATE GREENAWAY (c. 1884)

The genus Tulipa comprises about one hundred species, indigenous to an astoundingly wide geography. Tulips range naturally from Greece, Sardinia, Sicily, Algeria, and Italy through Iran, Iraq, Turkey, Tadzikistan and Armenia, on into Russia, northwestern China, the Tien Shan mountain range, and Japan. There is a word for "tulip" in practically every language of the world.

Our common name "tulip" comes from the Latin *Tulipa*, which in turn is a Latinized corruption of either the Turkish word for turban, *tulbend*, or its Arabic equivalent, *dulband*. The allusion of course, is to the shape of the flower. Tulips belong to the lily family; the Liliaceae also include such important kitchen produce as onions, garlic, shallots, and leeks; familiar garden bulbs such as lilies, fritillarias, and hyacinths; and beloved garden perennials such as hostas, daylilies, and liriopes.

Wild tulips (also known as species tulips) exist in a wide variety of sizes and colors, and will flower through a range of seasons. They tend to be more perennial and longer-lived than the Dutch hybrids, and have become extremely popular with amateur and professional gardeners alike. It is from the hybridization and selection of these wild tulips that modern cultivars arose. March-blooming *Tulipa turkestanica*, for example, is a dainty plant with butter yellow flowers that is native to Central Asia, especially the Tien Shan range. *Tulipa kaufmanniana* produces bicolored blossoms of yellow and red in April. It is indigenous to Central Asia, and has hybridized freely in the wild with *T. greigii*, *T. dubia*, and *T. tschimganica* to produce progeny with various colors, including combinations of red, pink, yellow, and white. Another Central Asian native is *T. fosteriana*, which possesses orange-red flowers with the familiar black blotch in the interior base of the petals.

Persian mythology tells of the ill-fated youth Farhad, who loved a beautiful maiden named Sharine (or Shirine). One day Farhad received a false message from an enemy telling him his beloved was dead (it is unclear whether the information originated with a suitor for Sharine's hand or a political rival of Farhad). The deceived and bereft Farhad promptly mounted his favorite horse and galloped straight off the nearest cliff. As the blood from his many wounds touched the earth, blood red tulips sprang forth (possibly thanks to the intervention of the powerful plant god Haoma).

Some ethnobotanists and botanical historians theorize that *Tulipa sharonensis*, the Sharon tulip—a wild red tulip that grows in the mountains of Iran—may be the "rose of Sharon" mentioned in the Song of Solomon. The Sharon tulip is native to Israel, particularly the Plain of Sharon, which lies between Carmel and Jaffa. However, most experts agree that the Old Testament refers to *Hibiscus syriacus*, the summer-flowering shrub we commonly know as the rose of Sharon.

Tulips have a long, rich history, which, unlike many popular garden flowers, did not begin in Europe; tulips do not appear in the medieval unicorn tapestries of England or France, they are not mentioned in Renaissance herbals, nor are they referred to in the plays of Shakespeare. Their illustrious chronicle begins in the nations that eventually comprised what we know as the Ottoman Empire; particularly Turkey, as well as Iran, Iraq, Syria, Jordan, and Israel. It was from these Middle Eastern countries that tulips were introduced to Europe—particularly notable was the squat, large-flowered *Tulipa armena*, as well as *T. humulis* and *T. julia*.

Tulip motifs have been discovered on ancient Middle Eastern pottery shards dating as far back as 2200 - 1600 BC. Their imagery has survived on border fragments of ninth-century Byzantine fabric. Within the thirteenth-century realm of Sultan Othman (or Osman), the tulip was the emblem of true and perfect love. As a floral messenger of amour, tulips were sent in bouquets and mentioned in ancient Iranian love poetry. Tulip patterns were used extensively in Turkish mosaics, appearing in the magnificent mosaic-covered private dining room of Sultan Ahmet III, as well as in a ceramic panel in the area known as the Courtyard of the Black Eunuchs. Both pieces survive in the famed Topkapi Museum in Istanbul. Although it is possible that tulips may have been cultivated much earlier, we do know that after the fifteenth century, they were grown in the private gardens of the Sultans Mehmet II and Suleyman the Magnificent by the *bostanci*, the royal gardeners.

It was Ogier Ghiselin de Busbecq, the Ambassador of the Holy Roman Empire to Sultan Suleyman the Magnificent, who was the first European to be captivated by the tulips growing in Constantinople in 1554. His friend, the Flemish botanist and physician Carolus Clusius (also known as Charles de l'Ecluse) procured tulip seeds for his friend and patron Johann Conrad von Gemmingen, the Prince Bishop of Eichstatt. The Bishop, who died in 1612, was intensely interested in botany and horticulture, and spent most of his adult life developing the extensive botanic gardens around his castle. Tulips were described growing there by 1561. It is likely that in about 1559, Clusius had also sent tulips to England. When he moved to Holland in 1593 to take a new position as Professor of Botany in Leyden, tulips were already known and appreciated there. Paintings of tulips as cut flowers dating from the sixteenth century hang in the Biblioteca Comunale dell'Archiginnasio in Bologna. In 1601, another former employer of Carolus Clusius, the Holy Roman Emperor Rudolf II, commissioned a remarkable illustrated botanical, biological, and entomological folio of the flora and fauna found within his extensive collections at the imperial castle in Prague. Tulips were profusely illustrated—these are some of the first European color renditions.

By the seventeenth century, after the economic fall of Antwerp and the Hanseatic League (a group of northern German merchant-states that included Bremen, Lubeck, and Hamburg), Amsterdam became the first center of bourgeois capitalism, the great international port of the north, and the banking capital of Europe. The rich silt-laden alluvial plains that made up much of the nation's geography, in combination with a winter climate tempered by the Atlantic Ocean, enabled Holland to also emerge as one of the great horticultural bastions of the Old World.

The establishment of the Dutch East India Company in 1602 marked the advent of an era of prosperity for The Netherlands. Raising tulips became a hobby for the extremely wealthy, who were able to maintain large gardens and a staff to care for them. Climatically and agronomically, tulips relished the Dutch environment. At that time tulips were available only in a few varieties: single colors, striped flowers, and "bizzares," which had petals that were yellow with red and/or purple flames or white flamed with purple.

In the early 1630s an aphid-transmitted virus (known as *Potyvirus*) was discovered to have an extraordinary visual effect on tulip petals. Formerly solid-colored petals would be produced with incredibly delicate feathering of white or cream. These so-called "broken" tulips created an unparalleled sensation, and took Holland (as well as France) by storm. They became known as "Rembrandt" tulips by virtue of their popularity with the Flemish still-life painter and his peers.

The *Potyvirus* was not entirely beneficial: in addition to weakening and eventually killing the plant, the virus' artistic influence on the flower was unpredictable, varying widely from plant to plant and from year to year. Bewitched by the possibilities, tulip growers became obsessed. No vase became too elaborate or flamboyant to hold these august flowers. Artisans created ornate vessels and tulip pagodas in blue Delft—some stood as tall as four feet (1.2m). The wealthy merchant class began to invest in tulip futures, and bulb prices soared astronomically. A single choice bulb could sell for 13,000 guilders—about US $6,250! Speculators invested their life savings under the assumption that instant fortunes could be acquired. Prices became so exorbitant that eventually tulip bulbs were sold by the pound—but most of the time the bulbs were still growing, so the investor would have to estimate the projected weight. This extraordinary hysteria became known as Tulipomania (also Tulip Mania or the Wind Trade).

The frenzied obsession that was Tulipomania lasted merely three years, from 1634 to 1637. This was the only time in history that a non-agricultural crop had such a profound financial influence on a country's economy. On February 3, 1637, the market collapsed; but it wasn't until April 27, 1637, that the bankrupt were instructed to seek safety from their creditors. Ultimately, because tulips were not a commodity, a relatively small portion of individual merchants and regents faced real financial ruin—accompanied by the enormous embarrassment brought on by their greed, much to the amusement of the lower classes.

During this period, a carefully regimented and documented breeding program had manifested innumerable hybrids and cultivars. These were categorized within a strict classification system reflecting flower form, period of bloom, and plant height.

CLASS I Duc Van Tol: 6" (15cm)

CLASS II Single Early: 9–16" (22.5–40cm)

CLASS III Double Early: 9–16" (22.5–40cm)

CLASS IV Mendel: 16–26" (40–65cm), resembling Darwins, blooming 2 weeks earlier

CLASS V Triumph: 16–26" (40–65cm), resembling Darwins, slightly earlier than Mendels

CLASS VI Cottage: all tulips not in other classes

CLASS VII Dutch Breeders: flowers oval or cupped; brown, purple, red or bronze; base white or yellow generally stained green or blue

CLASS VIII English Breeders: flowers forming a ⅓–½ hollow ball when expanded

CLASS IX Darwin: lower part of flower usually rectangular in outline

CLASS X Broken Dutch Breeders: Dutch Breeders with color feathered or striped due to genetics only, not viral infection

CLASS XI Broken English Breeders: color feathered or striped due to genetics only, not viral infection

CLASS XII Rembrandt: Darwin tulips with color feathered or striped due to genetics only, not viral infection

CLASS XIII Broken Cottage: cottage tulips with color feathered or striped due to genetics, not viral infection

CLASS XIV Parrot: varieties with slashed or fringed petals

CLASS XV Late Doubles

CLASS XVI Species and first crosses between species

Many archival, heirloom and antique varieties remain available commercially to the home gardener. One of the oldest by far is the archival Single Early 'Keizerskroon,' which dates back to 1750 in Holland. Some of the heirloom selections still available include the red-flowered Single Early Single tulip 'Van der Neer', dated about 1860; the Single Early 'La Tulipe Noire', the first "black" tulip, introduced in 1891 (named in honor of Alexandre Dumas' romantic novella of the same title; and the Early Single tulip 'Pink Beauty', which had its debut in 1889. Some of the extant antique introductions include the fragrant, orange-flowered Single Early 'General de Wet', selected in 1904, and lemon-yellow Single Late tulip 'Golden Harvest', which dates from 1928. In 1933, a remarkable creamy white tulip flamed with red was marketed as 'Cordell Hull'.

In addition to their illustrious history, dignified mythology, dizzying fragrance, and sheer splendor of color and form, tulips are edible. The bulbs of tulips are edible when cooked, and many cultures have made a habit of eating them. Floral parts, however, may be consumed raw. In China and Japan grows *Tulipa edulis* (its species name refers to the edible qualities of the bulb), which is roasted or stir-fried in these countries. Recently, the genus name was changed to Amana, but this does not alter its culinary attributes. Ancient Persian aphrodisiacal dishes include the almond oil-sautéed stamens and ovaries of tulip flowers. During the Second World War, many Nazi-threatened Dutch were forced to consume their tulip crops for sustenance. Adventurous cooks may use tulip flowers as edible chalices to hold cold seafood salads or other chilled tidbits. However, tulips contain a compound known as tulipalin-A, which may cause an allergic reaction in many people, so it's best to be cautious.

Today tulip-lovers worldwide enjoy them planted by the hundreds in botanic gardens or arboreta; flowering in the historic gardens of European chateaux, villas and castles; and blooming with subtle hues and voluptuous forms in our own gardens. We have discovered the joys of the diminutive wild species tulips, which are more free-flowering and perennial than the blowzy hybrids. With our incurred gardening maladies, which we lovingly call "weeder's knee," "planter's back," or "troweler's wrist," we enjoy these little gems planted in a shoulder-level rock wall bed or small rock garden—so that we may admire them without bending our tired joints. We've learned to pick them properly, so as not to sacrifice next years' blossoms, and have grasped how to force them indoors for winter enjoyment. Tulips will indeed accompany us throughout our gardening lives.

Tulipa semper augusta.
The tulip forever dignified.
Dutch saying (in Latin), c. 1630

The gardens fire with joyful blaze
Of Tulips in the morning's rays.

Ralph Waldo Emerson

The other thing I love is the way tulips
are their own arrangement,
stems and blossoms slowly turning and bending,
changing with each passing day.
Greenery, other flowers, all the arrangers'
embellishments only confuse the issue—
tulips—are always prettiest, I think,
without bother or fussiness.

Leslie Land

I was gazing at some tulips,
the supreme image in our clime of gayety in nature,
their globes of petals opening into chalices
and painted with spires of scarlet and orange
wonderously mingled with a careless freedom
that never goes astray.

Havelock Ellis

I always think that this, the time of Tulips,
is the season of all the year
when the actual arranging of flowers
affords the greatest pleasure.
The rush and heat of summer
have not yet come;
the days are still fairly restful,
and one is glad to greet and
handle these early blossoms.

Gertrude Jekyll

*Tulipase do carry so stately and delightful a form,
and do abide so long in their bravery,
that there is no Lady or Gentleman of any worth
that is not caught with this delight.*

John Parkinson

Nature rarer uses yellow
Than another hue;
Saves she all of that for sunsets,
Prodigal of blue.
Spending scarlet like a woman;
Yellow she affords
Only scantly and selectly,
Like a lover's words.

Emily Dickinson

In his garden every man may be his own artist without apology or explanation.

Louise Bebe Wilder

Delicious symphonies, like airy flowers
Budded, and swell'd , and full-blown, shed full showers
Of light, soft unseen leaves of sound divine.

John Keats

I do not love Tulips,
but I welcome them
very cordially in[to] my garden.
Others have loved them;
the Tulip has had her head
turned by attention.

Alice Morse Earle

We must have these gay, lovely, living goblets,
typical of spring days.
In broad patches of interesting combinations,
in long drifts in front of shrubberies,
and in beds near the house,
to be followed by annuals.

Anna Gilman Hill

A parrot tulip in the full blown stages is blowsiness personified.

Leslie Land

No more I spake, but thanked kind fate,
When Idleness the garden gate
Threw wide open, and unafraid
To that sweet spot quick entry made.

W. Lorns and J. Clopinel

Haarlem offered prizes for tulip-growing; and this fact brings us in the most natural manner to that celebration which the city intended to hold on May 15th, 1673, in honor of the great black tulip, immaculate and perfect, which should gain for its discoverer one hundred thousand gilders!

Alexandre Dumas

*To raise flowers is a common thing,
God alone gives them fragrance.*

Chinese Proverb

Yet rich as morn of many hue
When flashing clouds through the darkness strike,
The tulip's petals shine in dew
All beautiful, yet none alike.

Montgomery

Flowers seem intended for the solace
of ordinary humanity.

John Ruskin

O gallant flowering May,
Which month is painter of the world.

Unknown

*There is not a single colour hidden away
in the chalice of a flower...to which,
by some subtle sympathy
with the very soul of things,
my nature does not answer.*

Oscar Wilde

The tulips I had planted last autumn were in bloom, and I liked to sit and caress their petals, which felt disgustingly delicious, like scraps of peau de soie.

Jamaica Kinkaid

For love of flowers every blooming square
in cottage gardens seen
from the flying windows of the train
has its true and touching message for the traveller;
every bush and tree in nearer field and farther wood
becomes an object of delight and
stirs delightful thought.

Mrs. Francis King

As I beheld this beauty in flowers, I said to myself: "Here is an end to adjectives."

Mrs. Francis King

Oft in a flower love's secret hidden lies.

Marcelaine Desbordes-Valmore

Beholde, with lively heew, fair flowers
that shine so bright:
With riches, like the orient gems,
they paynt the molde in sight.
Beez, humming with soft sound,
(their murmer is so small)
Of blooms and blossoms suck the topps,
on dewed leaves they fall.

Tottell's Miscellany

Tall tulips lift in scarlet tire
Brimming the April dusk with fire.

Lizette Woodworth Reese

For winter's rains and ruins are over,
And all the seasons of snows and sins;
The days dividing loves and lover
The light that loses, the night that wins;
And time remembered is grief forgotten,
And forests are slain and flowers begotten;
And in the green underwood and cover
Blossom by blossom the spring begins.

Algernon Charles Swinburne

It is pleasant to think, just under the snow,
That stretches so bleak and blank and cold,
Are beauty and warmth that we cannot know —
Green fields and leaves and blossoms of gold.

Yes, under this frozen and dumb expanse,
Ungladdened by bee or bird or flower,
A world where the leaping fountains glance,
And the buds expand, is waiting its hour.

T. Hempstead

$\mathcal{M}$y spring appears,
Oh see what here doth grow.

Sir Philip Sydney

Rise up, my love, my fair one, and come away.

For, lo, the winter is past, the rain is over and gone;

The flowers appear on the earth…

—The Song of Solomon

I love old gardens best—
tired old gardens
that rest in the sun.

Henry Bellamen

When I was a boy,
I thought scent was contained
in dewdrops on flowers,
and if I got up very early in the morning,
I could collect it and make perfume.

Oscar de la Renta

Though not a whisper of her voice he hear,
The buried bulb does know
The signals of the year
And hails the Summer with his lifted spear.

Coventry Patmore

Love's language may be talked with these;
To work our choicest sentences
No blossoms can be meeter;
And such being used in Eastern bowers,
Young maids may wonder if the flowers
Or meanings be the sweeter.

Elizabeth Barrett Browning

The front yard was sacred to the best beloved [and] honored of garden flowers. The flowers were often of scant variety, but were those deemed the gentlefolk of the flower world—a few scarlet and single yellow tulips, and grape hyacinths.

Alice Morse Earle

But any man that walks the mead,
In bud, or blade, or bloom may find,
According as his humors lead,
A meaning suited to his mind.

Alfred, Lord Tennyson

I pushed the gate that swings so silently,
And I was in the garden and aware
Of early daylight on the flowers there
And cups of dew sun-kindled.

Paul Verlaine

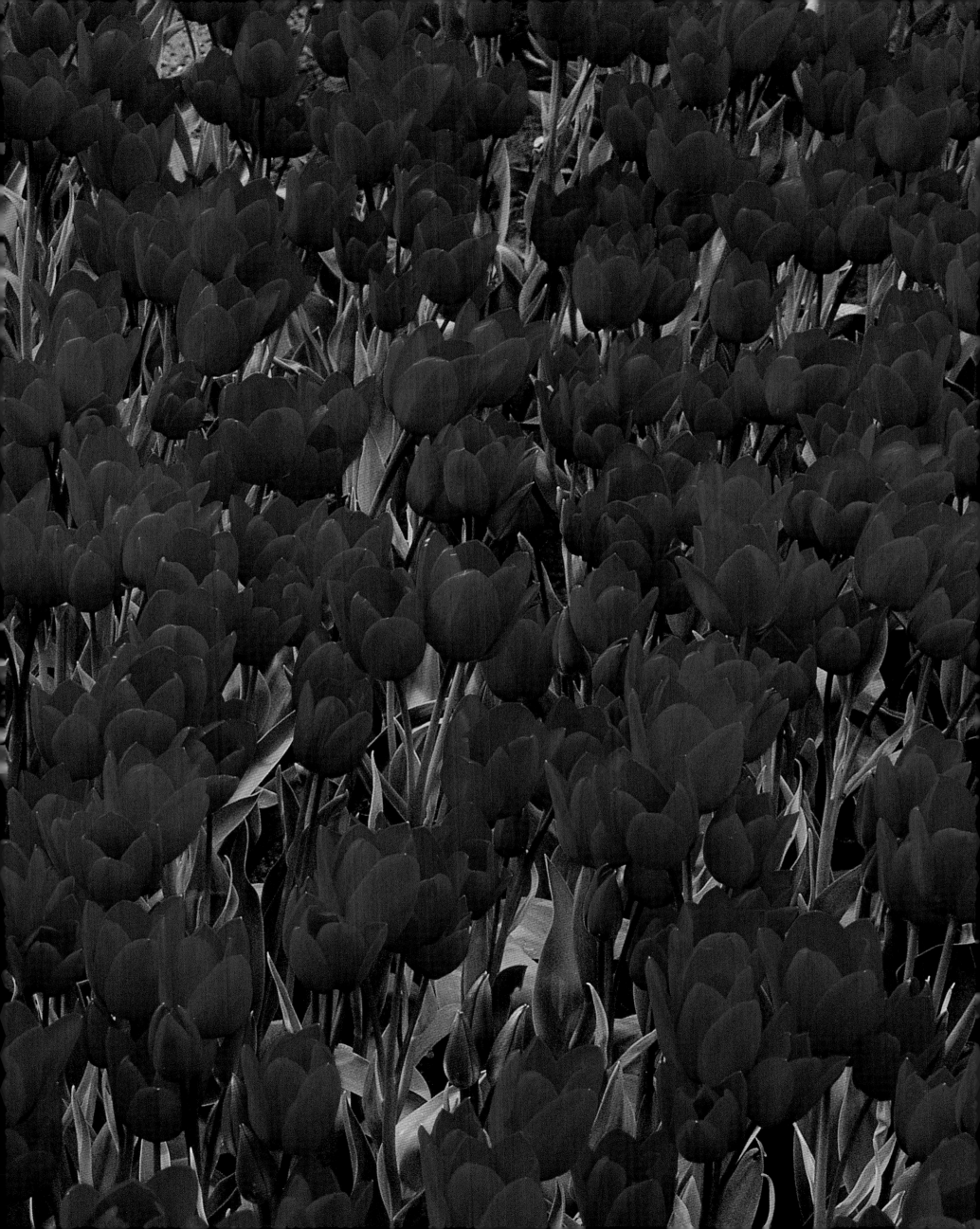

All night the small feet of the rain
About my garden ran;
Their rill-like voices called and cried
Until the dawn began.

Mrs. Shorter

And the spring arose on the garden fair,
Like the spirit of love felt everywhere;
And each flower and herb on earth's dark breast
Rose from the dreams of its wintry rest.

Percy Bysshe Shelley

I will be the gladdest thing under the sun!
I will touch a hundred flowers and not pick one.

Edna St. Vincent Millay

April appeared, the green earth's impulse came
Pushing the singing sap until each bud
Trembled with delicate life as soft as flame,
Filled with the mighty heart-beat as with blood.

Unknown

May, with alle thy floures and thy grene,
Welcome be thou, faire, fresshe May.

Geoffrey Chaucer

You convert it, let's say, into one of the sweetest gardens of the world—with spaces for spring bulbs, bursting out everywhere in lemon and scarlet, and gentian and ivory.

Henry Mitchell

Safe in the earth they lie, serenely waiting;
They never speak to north winds or to snow,
Perfume and color in the dark creating,
Fit for the sunlight world that they will know.

Louise Driscoll

Flowers.....have a mysterious and subtle
influence upon the feelings,
not unlike some strains of music.
They relax the tenseness of the mind.
They dissolve its rigor.

Henry Ward Beecher

*S*hed no tear! O shed no tear!
The flowers will bloom another year.
Weep no more! O weep no more!
Young buds sleep in the root's white core.

John Keats

To analyze the charms of flowers
is like dissecting music;
it is one of those things
which is far better to enjoy,
than to attempt to understand.

Henry Theodore Tuckerman

The butterfly is a flying flower,
The flower is a tethered butterfly.

Ecouchard Le Brun

And the Spring arose in the garden fair,
Like the Spirit of Love felt every where;
And each flower and herb on Earth's dark breast
Rose from the dreams of its wintery rest.

And the sinuous paths of lawn and of moss,
Which led through the garden along and across,
Some open at once to the sun and the breeze,
Some lost among bowers of blossoming trees.

Were all paved with daisies and delicate bells
As fair as the fabulous asphodels,
And flowers which drooping as day drooped too
Fell into pavilions, white, purple, and blue,
To roof the glow-worm from the evening dew.

Percy Bysshe Shelley

This bud of love, by summer's ripening breath,
May prove a beauteous flower when we next meet.

William Shakespeare

Earth laughs in flowers.

Ralph Waldo Emerson

Flowers nodding gaily, scent in air,
Flowers poised, Flowers for the hair,
Sleepy Flowers, Flowers bold to stare —
O pick me some!

T. Sturge Moore

The meanest flowers of the vale,
The simplest note that swells the gale,
The common sun, the air, the skies,
To him are opening paradise.

Thomas Gray

Of course everything is blooming most recklessly;
if it were voices instead of colors, there would be an
unbelievable shrieking into the heart of the night.

Rainer Maria Rilke

Who, that was blessed with parents that indulged themselves, and children with a flower garden, can forget the happy innocent hours spent in its cultivation! O! Who can forget those days, when to announce the appearance of a bud, or the coloring of a tulip, or the opening of a rose, or the perfection of a full-blown peony, was glory enough for one morning.

Joseph Breck

Gardens can link our souls with the divine.

William Howarf Adams

The garden, mimic of spring,
is gay with flowers.

Dorothy Wordsworth

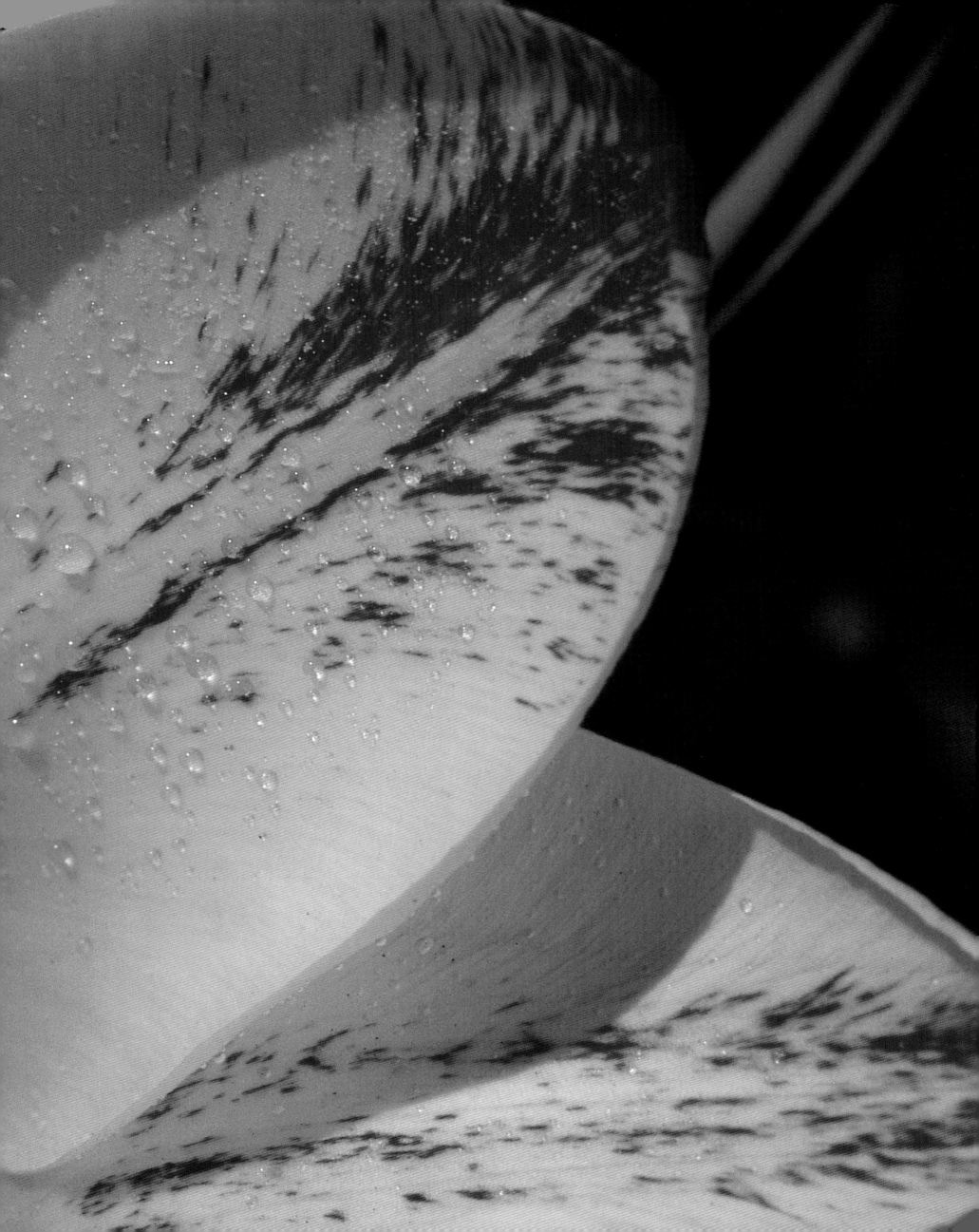

The snowdrop, and then the violet,
Arose from the ground with warm rain wet,
And their breath was mixed with fresh odour, sent
From the turf, like the voice and the instrument.

Then the pied wind-flowers and the tulip tall,
And narcissi, the fairest among them all,
Who gaze on their eyes in the stream's recess;
Till they die of their own dear loveliness.

Percy Bysshe Shelley

Around here, we call tulips the
"lipsticks of the garden"
because their rich colors and elegant flowers
give the spring border that final touch
that brings it to life.

Amos Pettingill

Furs fare you well, the Winter is quite gone
and beauty's quarter now is coming on.
When nature striveth most to show her pride
our beauty's being the cheefe we must not hide.

Wenceslaus Hollar

Sweet scents,
Are the swift vehicles of still sweeter thoughts;
And nurse and mellow the dull memory,
That would let drop without them her best stores.

Savage Landor

When the woods and groves are covered with green,
and grass and flowers appear in the orchards and meadows,
and the birds who were sad are now gay among the foliage,
then I also sing and exalt, I bloom again and flourish,
as is my wont.

Bernard de Ventadour

"*Oh, have pity, have mercy, sir!*"
said van Baerle, "don't take me away!
Let me look once more!
Is what I see down there the black tulip?
Quite black? Is it possible?"

Alexandre Dumas

See how the flowers, as at parade,
Under their colours stand displayed:
Each regiment in order grows,
That of the Tulip, pink and rose.

Andrew Marvell

I have a garden of my own,
Shining with flowers of every hue;
I love it dearly while alone,
But I shall love it more with you.

Thomas Moore

*When Holland went insane, a tulip bulb replaced
each brain. Speculation soared. Fortunes in florins
would afford merely a bulb. In shrieks, brokers bid,
paying dearly for "broken" petals of enflamed streaks.
Merchants offered the moon for one bulbil of
Zomerschoon and called it "sport" when mutations
might distort a Rembrandt's variegation. Everywhere
fast money was made though skeptics said such a
"Wind Trade" would never last, for the goddess Flora
and her fools made a folly of fiscal rules. And each
exotic tulip bearing an inflated price also bore a virus
transmitted by lice. When overnight the crash came,
no one dwelt on blight or blame. Fusing fantasy,
finance, and flowers still seemed better than other
worldly powers. Inasmuch, God blest the Dutch.*

Susan Kinsolving

S*till*
in a way
nobody sees a flower
really
it is so small
we haven't the time
and to see takes time
like to have a friend takes
time.

Georgia O'Keeffe

How well the skilful Gardener drew
Of flow'rs and herbs this Dial new;
Where from above the milder Sun
Does through a fragrant Zodiac run;
And, as it works, the industrious Bee
Computes its time as well as we.
How could such sweet and wholesome Hours
Be reckon'd but with herbs and flow'ers!

Andrew Marvell

A Gardener's Album! Ready in your hand,
For friends at home, or in some distant land;
Carrying a message, scented and aglow,
Of all the joys a garden can bestow.
Go, happy book, to capture and retain
These garden joys till summer comes again.

Reginald Arkell

Tulip Societies

The International Bulb Society
PO Box 4928
Culver City, CA 90230
Annual Dues: $30

Cottage Garden Society
c/o Mr. Clive Lane
Hurstfield House, 244 Edelston Road
Crewe, Cheshire, England, CW2 7 EJ
011-44-2702-50776

Helpful Organizations

Netherlands Flower Bulb Information Center
426 Henry Street
Brooklyn, New York 11231
718-693-7789

Tulip Time Information
Holland, Michigan
1-800-822-2770

Further Reading

Attenborough, David. *The Private Life of Plants*. Princeton University Press, Princeton, NJ. 1995.

Barker, Nicolas. *Hortus Eystettensis: The Bishops Garden*. Harry N. Abrams, Inc., New York. 1994.

Bronzert, Kathleen and Sherwin, Bruce (Editors). *The Glory of the Garden*. Produced by The Philip Leif Group, Inc. Avon Books, New York. 1993.

Clark, Kenneth. *Civilisation; A Personal View*. Harper & Row, New York. 1969.

Coco, Carla. *Secrets of the Harem*. The Vendome Press, New York and Paris. 1977.

Cook, Ferris. *Invitation to the Garden*. Stewart, Tabori & Chang, New York. 1992

Earle, Alice Morse. *Old-Time Gardens*. The MacMillan Company, London. 1901.

Greenaway, Kate. *Language of Flowers*. Gramercy Publishing Company, New York. 1884.

Hill, Anna Gilman. *Forty Years of Gardening*. Frederick A. Stokes Compan, New York. 1938.

Hendrix, Lee and Vignaux-Wilberg, Thea. *Nature Illuminated*. The J. Paul Getty Museum, Los Angeles. 1997.

Hinnells, John R. *Persian Mythology*. Peter Bedrick Books, New York. 1983.

Hughes, Holly (Compilation). *Gardens—Quotations on the Perennial Pleasuress of Soil, Seed and Sun*. Running Press, Philadelphia and London. 1994.

King, Mrs. Francis. *The Well-Considered Garden*. Charles Scribner's Sons, New York. 1915.

King, Mrs. Francis. *Variety in the Littlke Garden*. The Atlantic Monthly Press, Boston. 1923.

Kinsolving, Susan (Poems) and Colgan, Susan (Art). *Among Flowers*. Panache Press–Clarkson/Potter, New York. 1993.

Land, Leslie and Phillips, Roger. *The 3,000 Mile Garden*. Viking Press, New York. 1992.

Lloyd, Christopher. *The Well-Tempered Garden*. Random House, New York. 1973.

Lodewijk, Tom and Buchan, Ruth (Editor). *The Book of Tulips*. Vendome Press, New York. 1978

Martin, Laura. *Garden Flower Folklore*. The Globe Pequot Press, Chester, CT. 1987.

McGuire, Diane Kostral (Editor). A Horticulture Book: *American Garden Design*. MacMillan, New York. 1994.

Marranca, Bonnie (Editor). *American Garden Writing*. Penguin Books, New York. 1988

Okun, Sheila. *The Language of Flowers*. Harmony Books, New York. 1989.

Rockwell, F. F., and Grayson, Esther, C. *The Complete Book of Bulbs*. Doubleday & Company, Garden City, NJ. 1951.

Smith, A. W. *A Gardener's Book of Plant Names*. Harper & Row, Publisher, New York. 1963.

Strong, Roy. *A Celebration of Gardens*. Sagapress/Timber Press, Portland, Oregon. 1991.

Taylor, Paul. *Dutch Flower Painting: 1600–1720*. Yale University Press, New Haven & London. 1995.

Wright, Richardson. *The Gardener's Bed-Book*. J. B. Lippincott Company, Philadelphia and London. 1929.

Tulip Identification Guide

Photo Credits

©Roger Foley: pp. 8–9, 17, 21, 59, 69, 84-85, 108-109, 141, 161

The Garden Picture Library: ©Linda Burgess: p. 117; ©Chris Burrows: pp. 25, 43, 79, 83, 87, 123, 127, 144–145, 147, 169; ©Rex Butcher: pp. 1, 57, 149; ©Jan Ceravolo: p. 67; ©Neil Holmes: pp. 4–5, 6, 96-97, 113, 171, 173; ©Ute Klaphake: pp. 53, 131; ©Lamontagne: pp. 71, 111; ©Marianne Majerus: pp. 132–133; ©Howard Rice: pp. 15, 37, 120–121; ©Friedrich Strauss: p. 93; ©Brigitte Thomas: p. 137; ©Juliette Wade: p. 81; ©Steven Wooster: pp. 103, 129

©John Glover: pp. 22–23, 31, 33, 49, 65, 77, 89, 99, 105, 107, 119, 135, 143, 153

©Anne Gordon: p. 45

©Dency Kane: pp. 2, 3, 13, 34–35, 39, 46–47, 51, 60–61, 63, 72–73, 125, 139, 151, 159, 163, 166–167

Clive Nichols Garden Pictures: ©Clive Nichols: pp. 27, 41 (Chenies Manor, Bucks), 75, 91 (Keukenhof, Holland), 95, 101, 115, 156–157 (Keukenhof, Holland); ©Graham Strong: p. 19

©Steve Terrill: pp. 55, 155, 165

MetroBooks

An Imprint of the Michael Friedman Publishing Group, Inc.

First MetroBooks Edition 2002

Library of Congress Cataloging-in-Publication Data Available Upon Request.

ISBN 1-58663-550-6

Editor: Susan Lauzau
Art Director: Jeff Batzli
Designer: Jennifer Markson
Photography Editor: Wendy Missan
Production Managers: Camille Lee and Leslie Wong

Color separations by Colourscan Co Pte Ltd
Printed in Singapore by CS GRAPHICS Pte, Ltd.

1 3 5 7 9 10 8 6 4 2

For bulk purchases and special sales, please contact:
Michael Friedman Publishing Group, Inc.
Attention: Sales Department
230 Fifth Avenue
New York, NY 10001
212/685-6610 FAX 212/685-3916

Visit our website:
www.metrobooks.com